The ADVENTURES of

Peighten & Gingerbread

Navigating Cancer Diagnosis and Developing Coping Strategies for Grief

Book 1

Written by Feryn Heath, LT

Illustrated by Carla and James Ramos

To request permission, contact the publisher at:
publisher@innerpeacepress.com

ISBN: 978-1-958150-39-9
The Adventures of Peighten and Gingerbread: Navigating Cancer Diagnosis and Developing Coping Strategies for Grief

First publication: October 2024

Published by **Inner Peace Press**
Eau Claire, Wisconsin, USA
www.innerpeacepress.com

DEDICATION

This story is dedicated to my loving and resolute parents, Robin and Keith Spotleson, who were taken too soon after their individual battles with cancer.

This story is additionally dedicated to my daughters, Peighten and Kinsley. Peighten, I hope this story helps you understand that you are not alone in your grief. Kinsley, the namesake of your grandmother, you brought joy to our family during one of our darkest hours. My wish is for both of you to follow your dreams and change the world with your beautiful hearts and minds.

Lastly, this book is dedicated to my family and mentors. Thank you for believing in me and for encouraging me to take a leap of faith.

* GLOSSARY WORDS

Look at the back of the book for definitions and more information of harder/new words.

My parents gave me Gingerbread after I lost my grandma to help with my **GRIEF**.

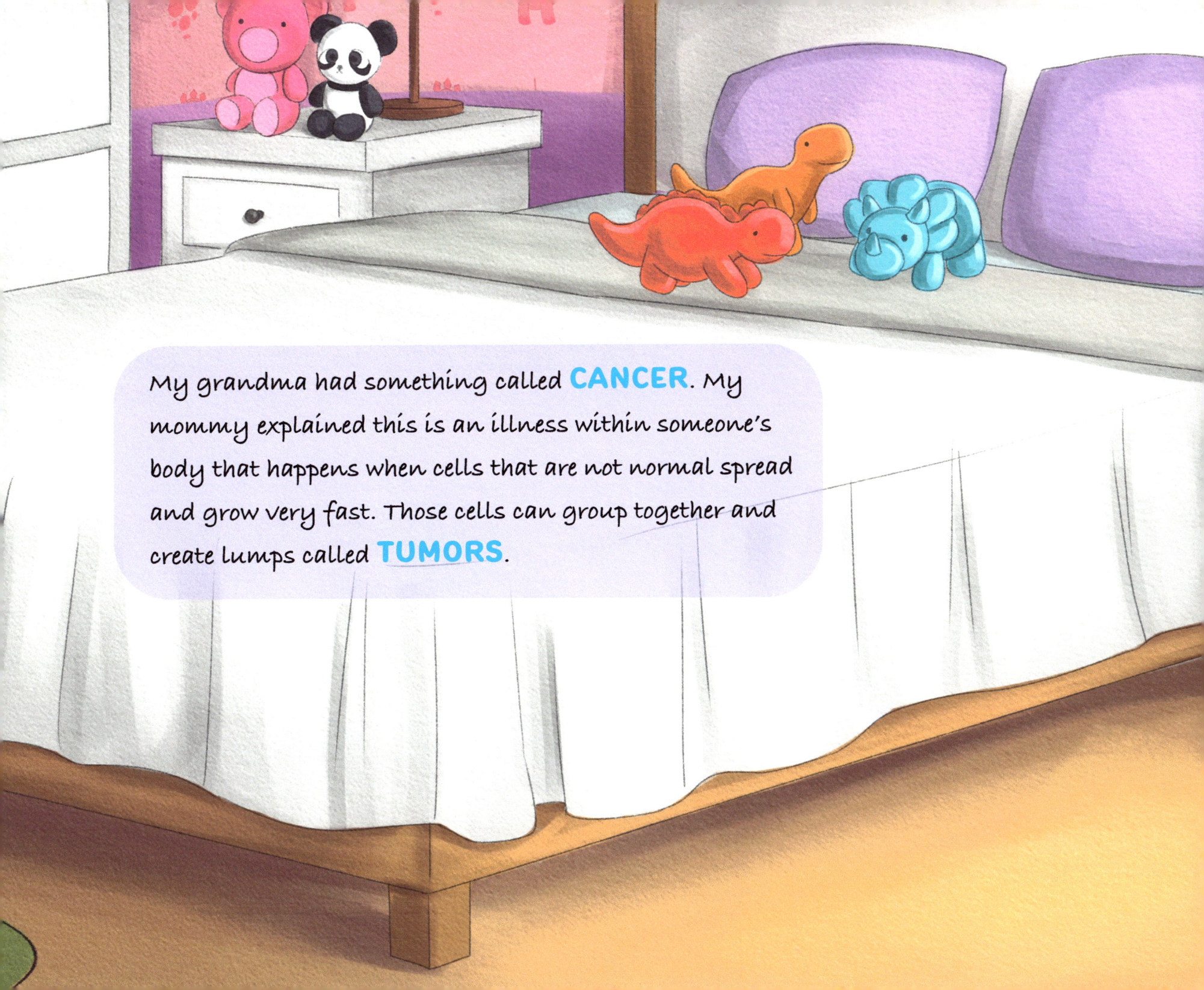

My grandma had something called **CANCER**. My mommy explained this is an illness within someone's body that happens when cells that are not normal spread and grow very fast. Those cells can group together and create lumps called **TUMORS**.

When cancer is found, it can be treated with surgery, **CHEMOTHERAPY** medications, or **RADIATION THERAPY**. When cancer is found and treated early, many people are able to be **CURED**.

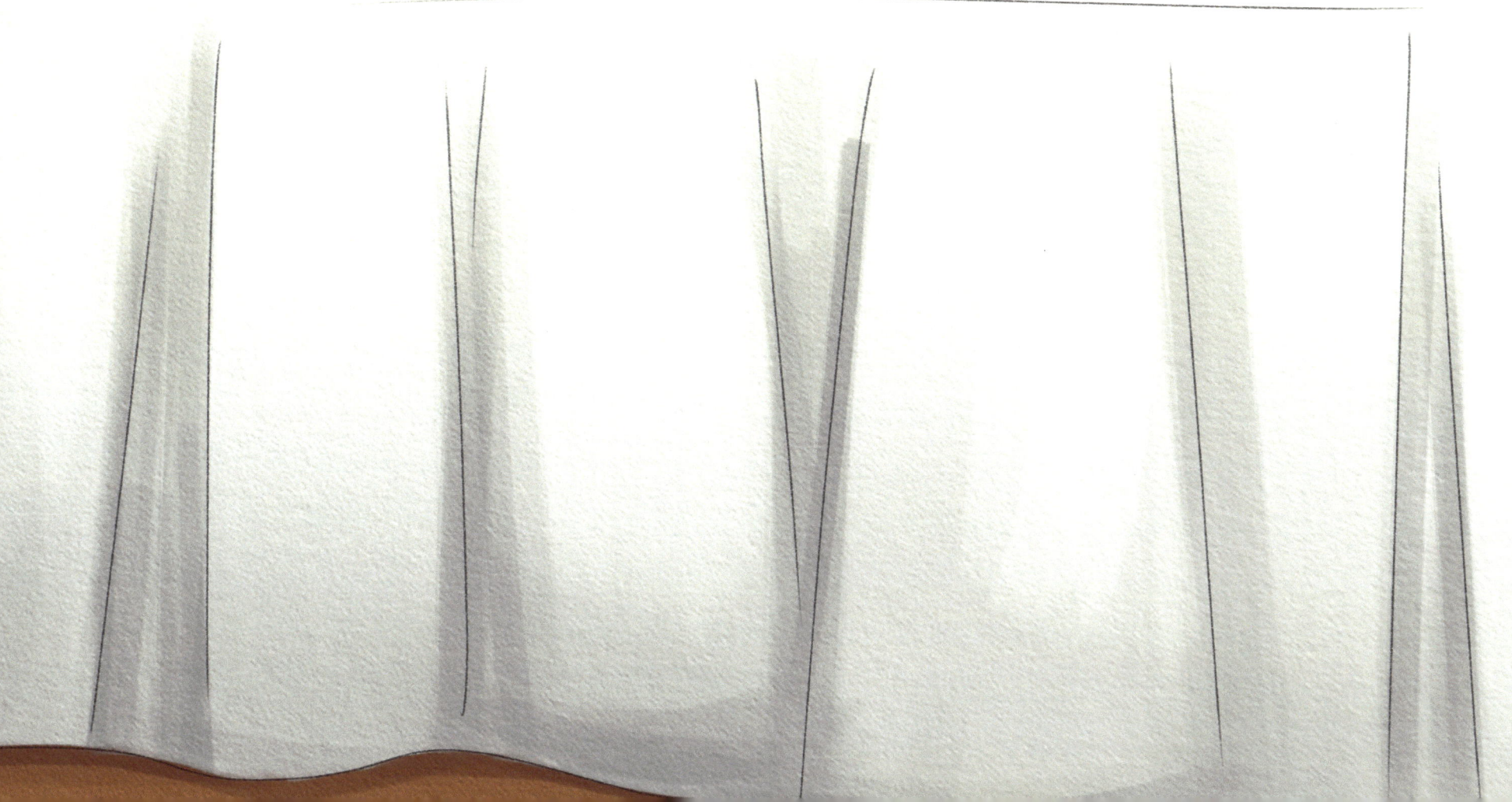

My grandma's cancer was called **TERMINAL**, which meant her body would not get better.

One morning, her body stopped working. Her heart stopped beating and she stopped breathing. Her brain stopped thinking and she no longer felt any pain.

I started to feel different. Sometimes I had nightmares and I would wake up frightened and scared.

Some days I would feel happy, but other days I would feel angry or sad.

My mommy explained that what I was feeling was something called **GRIEF**.

Grief is something that does not follow a timeline, but is a process that happens over time. Grief can be a sadness in your heart that shows when someone you love dies.

Grief is a normal process that happens when someone you love dies. Grief can cause a range of different emotions, and all of them are normal. With grief, your loved one is not physically here any more, but can be remembered and visited in your mind and in your heart.

I like to talk about and draw pictures of memories I had with my grandma. We had fun playing dress up and eating lunch at the park.

Echoes & Reactions:

Reflection of the day:

I have started to journal every night. I like to write poems and songs. I also write about the feelings I felt during the day.

I also started a scrapbook with my mommy. In it I get to use my creativity to decorate the pages with stickers, glitter, and my favorite pictures that remind me of my grandma.

I like when I get to hear my mommy tell me stories about my grandma. Mommy also answers all the questions I have about Grandma.

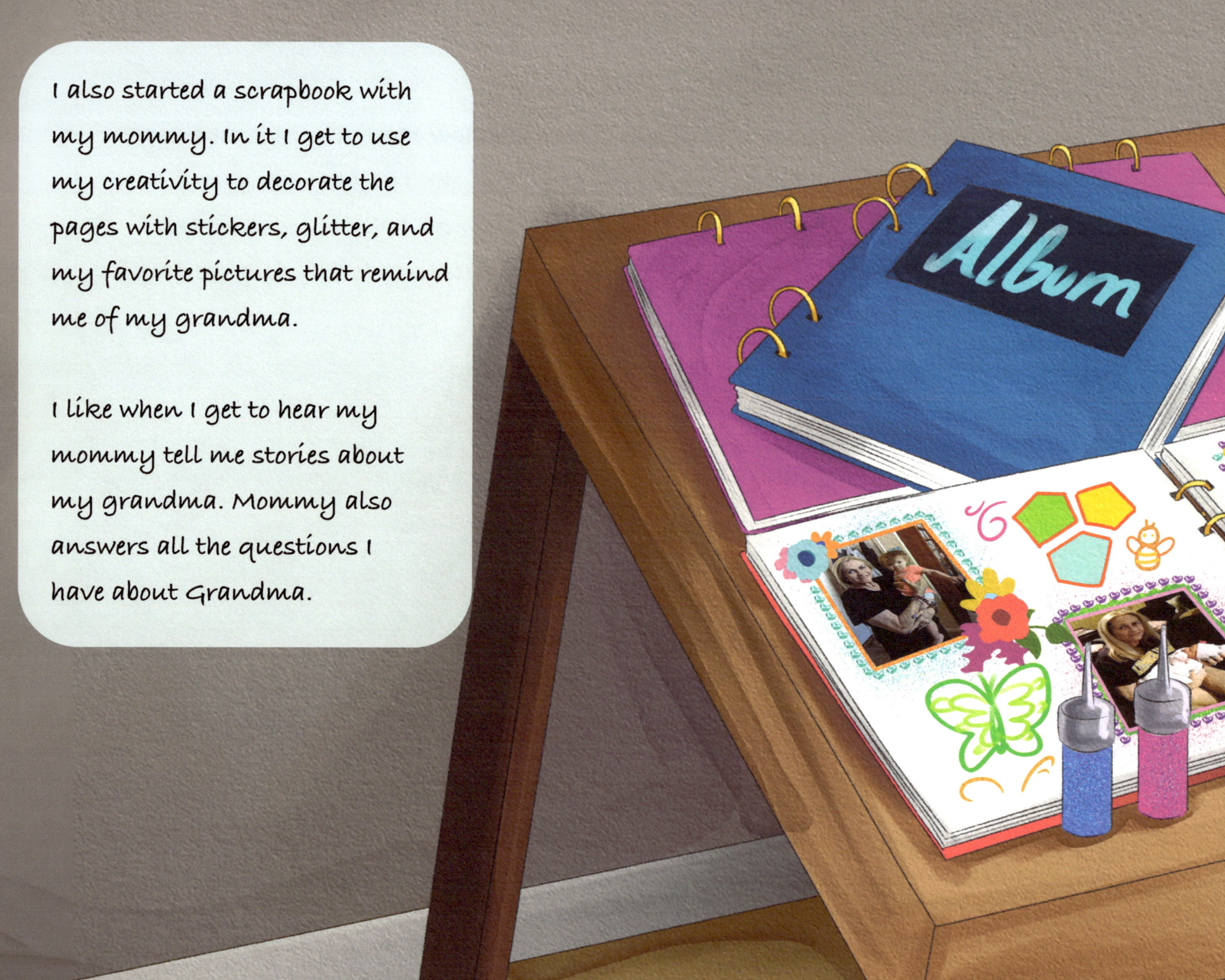

Through my grief I have learned that even though my grandma is gone, I can still love and remember her. I have both good and bad days, and I still miss my grandma every day. I've learned to treasure the moments I had with her and the activities that help me remember her.

Visit PeightenAndGingerbread.com
to discover more books by Feryn Heath

GLOSSARY WORDS

CANCER

Cancer refers to a group of diseases characterized by the uncontrolled growth and spread of abnormal cells. If not controlled, cancer can invade surrounding tissues and spread to other parts of the body through the bloodstream and lymphatic system. There are many different types of cancer, often named for the organ or type of cell in which they start.
Source: National Cancer Institute. (2021). Cancer. Retrieved from https://www.cancer.gov/about-cancer/understanding/what-is-cancer

CHEMOTHERAPY

Chemotherapy is a type of cancer treatment that uses drugs to kill cancer cells. It works by targeting cells that grow and divide quickly, which is characteristic of cancer cells. Chemotherapy may be used alone or in combination with other treatments such as surgery, radiation therapy, or immunotherapy.
Source: American Cancer Society. (2023). Chemotherapy. Retrieved from https://www.cancer.org/cancer/cervical-cancer/treating/chemotherapy.html

CURED

In the context of cancer, "cured" means that there are no signs of cancer after treatment and the patient is expected to remain free of cancer for the rest of their life. However, doctors may hesitate to use the term "cure," as it can be difficult to guarantee that cancer will never return.
Source: American Society of Clinical Oncology. (2023). What does it mean to be cured of cancer? Retrieved from https://www.cancer.net/navigating-cancer-care/cancer-basics/what-does-it-mean-be-cured-cancer

GRIEF

Grief is the emotional response to a significant loss, particularly the loss of a loved one. It involves various stages, including denial, anger, bargaining, depression, and acceptance. While the experience of grief is unique to each individual, it is typically marked by feelings of sadness, longing, and emotional distress.
Source: American Psychological Association. (2023). Grief. Retrieved from https://www.apa.org/topics/grief

RADIATION THERAPY

Radiation therapy is a form of cancer treatment that uses high doses of radiation to kill cancer cells or shrink tumors. It works by damaging the DNA inside the cancer cells, which prevents them from growing and dividing. It can be delivered externally through a machine or internally by placing radioactive material near the cancer cells.
Source: National Cancer Institute. (2022). Radiation therapy. Retrieved from https://www.cancer.gov/about-cancer/treatment/types/radiation-therapy

TERMINAL

A terminal illness refers to a disease or condition that is expected to lead to the death of the patient, typically within a limited time frame, often measured in months. Terminal cancer refers to cancer that cannot be cured or treated successfully and will result in the patient's death.
Source: National Institute on Aging. (2021). End of life: Helping with comfort and care. Retrieved from https://www.nia.nih.gov/health/end-life-helping-comfort-and-care

TUMOR

A tumor is an abnormal mass of tissue that forms when cells grow and divide more than they should or do not die when they should. Tumors can be benign (non-cancerous) or malignant (cancerous). Malignant tumors have the potential to invade and destroy surrounding tissue and spread to other parts of the body.
Source: Mayo Clinic. (2023). Tumor. Retrieved from https://www.mayoclinic.org/diseases-conditions/tumor/symptoms-causes/syc-20351688

Companion Journal
&
Therapeutic Workbook

This Book Belongs to:

_____

Dedicated to the memory of:

_____

ARTS AND CRAFTS WITH PEIGHTEN AND GINGERBREAD

Activities to be done individually or with grown-up assistance.

Maze Activity

Find your way to Grandma's heart.

Memorial Corner

Frame photos and mementos that remind you of your loved one and place them in a specially chosen space in your home.

Connect-the-Dots

Find Grandma's favorite animal and Peighten's favorite toy:

Memorial Rock Garden

Paint rocks with different words or pictures that remind you of your loved one who has died. Once all of the rocks have been decorated, create a shape of a heart/circle/square out of the rocks in your yard. With guardian assistance and approval, add a plant to the middle of the memorial rock garden: a small tree or flowers would work great!

PRO TIP: Put a layer of "modge podge" on all of the decorated rocks to help keep them from getting ruined outside by the weather.

Memory Treasure Chest

Create a treasure box of memories of your passed loved one. Decorate a shoe box, craft box, or any other item that contains a lid, with items that will make it unique. Use any material you like: paint, glitter, stickers, and gems are some examples. Once decorated, fill the box with items that remind you of your passed loved one and will remind you during moments of grief of the love your experienced by your loved one. Suggested storage: Store the "Memory Treasure Chest" in a place that is easy to access for moments of experienced grief. It is meant to be used as often as it helps.

Grief Genie Jar ~ Healing through Loss

We may not see a decrease in our grief over time, but we do change and grow in our ability to cope with it.

In this project, our grief is the heart. The ability for coping is the genie jar. The grief does not shrink, but we change as the genie jar grows.

Add items to the genie jar that might encourage growth. These could include people, places, objects, interests, hobbies, and talents.
All your answers are correct!

Now:
(grief is big)

In the Future:
(grief feels smaller when using positive coping strategies)

Poetry
Memories
Gymnastics
Gingerbread
Puppy shows
Journaling
Volunteering
Baby
Rock
Garden
Sister
Ballet
Reading
Therapy

Fill YOUR Genie Jar!

"Carry You with Me" Craft

Using materials like beads and string, create a bracelet or a necklace that reminds you of your loved one.

Using beads that have letters will allow you to spell out the name of the loved one who has died or a word that makes you think of them.

Attach a "split key ring" circular metal to turn your beaded creation into a key chain for your backpack!

CALMING YOGA POSES

Yoga poses can help with grief to let the sadness out through your body. Take your time with each posture and focus on even breathing: even in, even out.

 Child's Pose- Take a few deep breaths while sitting on your heels, lowering your forehead gradually to rest on the floor in front of your knees. Place your arms beside your body.

 Camel- Stand on your knees. Lift your heart and start to look up while you bring your hands to your ankles. Take two deep breaths and then slowly come back up.

 Warrior 2- Step one foot back from a standing position with the foot pointing slightly outwards. Raise your arms parallel to the floor, bend your front knee, and direct your eyes ahead, over the fingertips of your outstretched arm.

 Downward Dog- Bend over and place your palms flat on the ground while still standing. With your buttocks raised high, form an upside-down V by stepping your feet back. Keep your back straight, your heels reaching to the floor, and gaze between your legs.

 Extended Side Angle- From Warrior 2 bring your front hand to the inside of your front foot, and reach your other hand toward the ceiling. Repeat on the other side.

 Tree- Place the sole of one foot on the inner thigh of the other leg. Bend your knee and maintain your balance while standing on one leg. Move with the rhythm of a tree on a windy day. If you feel stable, reach your hands up overhead.

Cat/Cow pose- Get down on all fours with your wrists under your shoulders and your knees under your hips. Inhale while you look up - arch your back, lift your heart forward, and push your butt into the air for "cow" pose. Exhale as you look down towards your knees, rounding your spine up to arch your back, and press your chin into your chest for "cat" pose. Move between cat and cow with your breath.

Boat pose- Legs raised, keep a balanced position on your buttocks. Reach your hands away from you. Like a boat, rock in the sea

Cobra- Lay flat on your stomach, press into your hands, raise your head and shoulders off the floor, and release a snake-like hiss.

Bow- Lie belly down on the floor. Bend your knees and lift your feet up into the air. Push down on the floor with your hands, OR reach your hands back and grab your ankles. As you breathe, notice your body rocking in a bow.

Forward Fold- Starting from a standing position and keeping your back straight, bend forward at your hips, reaching your fingers to the floor. You may also reach for your toes or try to put your fingertips under your toes.

Lotus- Sit with criss cross legs, and bring your palms together. Close your eyes, and focus on your even breath. If your mind wanders, simply count your breaths, in and out.

Memory Grid

Decorate each of the squares with a memory or a symbol that reminds you of your loved one who has died. You may draw, or write, or even glue pictures on your grid. Use squares to write out the name of your loved one, or what you loved about them. Make your grid special for you and your loved one.

ONCE UPON A TIME... WRITING PROMPTS

Use this and the following pages to write your thoughts, or write more in your own journal.

Write about a favorite memory with your loved one who has passed.

Write about an item that helps you remember your loved one and any memories attached to that item.

Write about another time in your life where you experienced sadness and the ways in which you were able to overcome it.

"When I was around you, the emotions that I experienced were..."

"What I miss most about you is..."

"Things that I can do to honor your memory are...."

"I have grief because...."

"A lesson you taught me that I will never forget is..."

"My favorite activity that we would do together was...."

"If you were here, something I think you would tell me is..."

"Something that I wish I could ask you is..."

"Something that makes me think about you is..."

"The things I miss the most about you and our relationship are..."

"What has been the hardest part about you being gone for me has been..."

The coping skills that I can use to help me with my grief are...

Write a letter to your loved one.

Draw a picture of your loved one.

Interview family and friends to collect facts about your loved one who has died. Use the information from the interviews to write a story or a "biography" about your loved one.

POETRY

Writing poetry can help to express your feelings. Try the following poem types.

Lune Poem

Rules of the poem: This type of poem is made of three lines with a total of 11 words.

Line one- Three words

Line two- Five words

Line three- Three words

Example:

I miss you.

My heart needs a band-aid.

I love you.

My Lune Poem

Cinquain Poem

Rules of the poem: This type of poem contains five lines. The first line of the poem is the poem topic. The remaining four lines describe the chosen topic.

Line one- topic, one noun

Line two- two adjectives

Line three- three action words ending in -ing

Line four- four feelings or word phrases

Line five- one synonym of your topic

Example:

Angel

Wings, Halo

Flying, Moving, Fluttering

Happy, Glad, Safe, Cheerful

Spirit

My Cinquain Poem

Acrostic Poem

Rules of the poem: This type of poem requires that the first letter each line be capitalized and form a word, which is the subject of the poem.

Example:

"Grandma"

Gave the Best Hugs.

Red Robin was her nickname.

Always was on time for the tea parties I hosted.

Nostalgic stories and photos shared by mom.

Devoted to attending my activities and recitals.

Magical fun when we would use our imagination.

Always in my memories and forever loved in my heart.

My Acrostic Poem

THERAPEUTIC PROMPTS
To be done with a licensed therapist.

What is Sand Tray Therapy?
A mix between art and play therapy, "sand tray therapy" is a tool used by therapists that allows one to show their emotions with miniature objects instead of using their words.

Sand Tray Exercise Prompts (for therapist)
» Make a sand tray that shows symptoms and feelings of grief for your loved one who has died.
» Make a sand tray that shows your favorite memory with your loved one who has died.

» Make a sand tray that shows how you calm down when you are mad or sad.

» Make a sand tray that shows positive ways you can show your feelings to others.

» Make a sand tray that shows the love you felt by your loved one.

» Make a sand tray for the feeling of "hope."

» Make a sand tray for the feeling of "grief."

» Make a sand tray showing the funeral of your loved one who has died.

» Make a sand tray that shows your life before and after the death of your loved one.

» Make a sand tray that shows your family after the death of your loved one.

About the Author

Feryn Heath is a licensed therapist in the state of Arizona. Professionally, she works in the field of addiction, specializing working with individuals who struggle with process and/or substance addictions. Feryn, mom to two young daughters, wanted to use her passion for writing to create a book series that they would enjoy, while also being able to use her therapy background to teach children coping skills. Grief and loss have left an imprint on the author's life through the loss of her only sibling Justin in a commercial airline crash and through the loss of her parents, who both lost their individual battles with cancer. Feryn's goal for this book is to provide children with knowledge on grief and loss while additionally providing them with therapeutic resources that can be implemented to assist with the pain that can accompany grief so they are less likely to find themselves on the path of addiction and/or self harming.

About the book series

In the picture book series created for young readers ages 3-9, Peighten and her sidekick puppy Gingerbread educate readers about difficult topics, such as cancer, death, dementia, and grief. Peighten and Gingerbread provide readers with coping strategies to assist children in their range of feelings and emotions brought up from each story and through the included therapeutic activity pages at the end of each book.

www.ingramcontent.com/pod-product-compliance
Lightning Source LLC
Chambersburg PA
CBHW040820120626

46551CB00005B/610